AT THE SWEET HOUR OF HAND IN HAND

AT THE SWEET HOUR OF HAND IN HAND

by Renee Vivien

TRANSLATED FROM THE FRENCH
WITH AN INTRODUCTION BY

SANDIA BELGRADE

FOREWORD BY EDITOR AND COLLABORATOR

BONNIE POUCEL

THE NAIAD PRESS, INC.
1979

First published in Paris by Alphonse Lemerre as
A l'heure des mains jointes. poésies. 1 vol.

Printed in the United States of America
First Edition

Cover illustration by Tee A. Corinne

ISBN: 0-930044-11-8

Library of Congress Catalog Card Number LC 79-84859

Renée Vivien

SANDIA'S DEDICATION:

To the Mother

PUBLISHER'S NOTE

This is the second volume of the poetry of Renée Vivien in translation to be published by The Naiad Press. Unlike the first,* which was a selection of poems from the five separate collections Vivien left, this is a translation of an entire collection, perhaps the most important one.

The translator and her editor have stated in their forewords the motives and methods adopted in their presentation of these poems in English.

**The Muse of the Violets*, poems by Renee Vivien, translated from the French by Margaret Porter and Catharine Kroger. The Naiad Press, 1977.

ACKNOWLEDGMENTS

To the women all over the country who helped link me to the manuscript after much searching.

To the women of *Big Mama Rag*, who in their August 1973 issue printed an article by Liz Matthews on Vivien and Natalie Clifford Barney. Liz translated two poems and made some insightful observations that so haunted me, I almost had no choice from then on. At that point I promised myself I would go anywhere and do anything to be able to translate one of Renée Vivien's works. After some intermediary help from the Denver Public Library and the Library of Congress, Judy Grahn made the final connection to She-Bar Windstone, who provided the manuscript.

To Jeannette Foster, who, during the time I waited for the manuscript, inspired me with her book *Sex Variant Women in Literature*. She was the only one at that time offering me any in-depth analysis of Vivien and her work.

To Mrs. Quintana at the Espanola Public Library in New Mexico, who trusted me with the French dictionaries.

Thank you, Gypsy, for the *Petite Larousse*.

Thank you, Karobi, for xeroxing.

Thank you, Yarrow and Deann, for giving me and my typewriter shelter those last hectic months so we had space and time to midwife this book.

Lastly and most of all to Bonnie, my editor, who has always seemed like manna to me, a gift from the Mother, who had everything essential for the task: a bilingual woman with the eye and sensitivity of a poet and the patience and discipline of a Capricorn. Bonnie not only helped with word choices and syntax, but she also caught "Vivien fever" as I had. Once I wrote her saying that I thought I was being used for the work and that I felt like a vessel for Vivien to come through: she responded with this poem:

Surrounded
each daybreak
by sheaves of distilled
passion and pain
I vibrate with discovery
of a woman
whose life force
touches mine . . .
And the spark
falling on my longing
leaps into flame.

Sandia:
a vessel, yes!
but how did you calm
your racing heart
long enough
to take the
word
by
word?

–Sandia

May, 1979

About the translator:

It took Renée Vivien and 39 years of creative survival to get my first book published–though I have been writing for over 10 years and have two books of my own poetry completed (*New Moon in Her* and *Children of the Second Birth*) but not published yet, a novel in process, and an essay book in the wings.

I still remember unconsciousness and the first woman to break through the fog (Adrienne Rich) and the succession of friends and lovers and writers who followed. I can imagine where it is all leading.

I am a mental Aries who loves to live in the body. A vegetarian bear who misses the haunts of New Mexico. An M.A. who had to return to Denver where there are libraries, audiences, other women writers and artists. I began the Denver chapter of the Feminist Writers' Guild this Spring to try and heal the splits. As usual, I have found that we are our solutions as well as our dreams.

–Sandia

RENEE VIVIEN

CHRONOLOGY

1877– Born Pauline Tarn in Hawaii

1890– Meets Violet Shilleto, an intense though short-lived companion. The quasi-religious lover relationship follows Vivien all her life.

1898– Goes to Paris to live. Meets Natalie Clifford Barney, who is to be her most important love relationship. Barney is the Loreley of the lilies, and for Vivien her grand passion.

1901– Violet becomes sick and dies. Vivien and Barney split up.

1902– *Cendres et poussières; Brumes de fjords*
Vivien begins a relationship with Helene Van Zuylen de Nyevelt. Their joint writing is published under the name Paule Riversdale.

1903– *Evocations; Sappho; Du vert au violet; La Vénus des aveugles*

1904– Vivien and Barney go to Lesbos briefly, thinking to revive a Sapphic community and their relationship. Both fail.
Etudes et préludes; Kitharèdes; La dame à la louve; Le Christ; Aphrodite et M. Pépin; Une femme m'apparut

1906– *A l'heure des mains jointes*

1908– *Sillages; Flambeaux éteints*

1909– Vivien dies.

1910– *Dans un coin de violettes; Le vent des vaisseaux; Haillons*

FORWARD: ATTIRE-MOI, RENEE

The Process:

Although my job was principally to catch any misreadings of the French and to make the appropriate corrections, I discovered much about the process involved in translating and in women collaborating. This experience, as well as my own personal involvement, is what I would like to share.

One difficult problem in translating poetry is knowing how far to go or when to stop. After working over every poem with Sandia, I was ready for us to begin all over again, weighing the decisions, incorporating what we'd learned from each other, smoothing rough passages, getting suggestions from others (Diane's were always helpful). Fortunately for the ultimate completion, Sandia brought limits to my endless dissatisfaction.

I also saw my usefulness–with Sandia's confidence in me–in legitimizing departures from the literal version in order to retain the essence even while smoothing out the reading. One case in point was the phrase "*épanouie ainsi qu'une grenade*" in the poem "After Swinburne." Literally the words mean "expand like a grenade," but grenade in English just doesn't make it: its warlike image doesn't fit a love poem nor does it express the sense of a woman. Part of the process of translation was to give us together the courage to change the original, which we might have been less open to, working alone. Feeling uneasy with the word *grenade*, we checked the etymology and found that grenade is derived from the same source as the word *pomegranate.* The sense and sound of a pomegranate blossoming we felt expressed the meaning needed for an English translation without distorting Renée's original intent–and always *that* consideration was the basis for our decisions.

While all of Renée's verses contain a rhyming pattern, clearly this rhyme could not always be rendered in English. However, with some poems constructed in couplets, the more one got "inside" the lines, the more it became evident that her word choice was heavily influenced by the need to rhyme. Therefore, with some poems we attempted to keep a degree of rhyme, through changes in word order or other slight modifications that fully respected the meaning.

In some cases, rhyme can even be seen as part of the message of a poem. For instance, "*Confidence devant le soir*" expresses the contradiction "my love was so beautiful / it was very painful." The rhyming underlines and sets off the juxtaposition of feelings, perhaps even implying irony.

We made other working decisions. Most often we chose to keep the original French expressions for terms of endearment. "*Ma douce*" is a case in point: the word *douce* can mean softness, sweetness, calmness, or kindness: to limit its translation to a saccharine "my sweet" seemed a real distortion. Not to mention the phrase "*ma maîtresse*" and what a literal translation would render, given the implications of the word *mistress* in English.

So connotations and imagery were vital considerations. We tried to faithfully reproduce Vivien's extraordinary sense of imagery whenever possible. Our departures reflect the changes in signs and values and symbols from 1906 to 1977. Phrases that at the turn of the century connoted one thing have a totally different flavor today, especially if translated by substituting an equivalent word. We didn't want poetic license to become translator's license. One example might help here. In "*Psappha revit*" there is the line "*A qui l'or éternel des mondes fut donne . . .* ," which means "to whom the eternal gold of worlds was given." Taken word for word the phrase loses the sense Vivien intended, which we translated as "For whom a whole new world has opened up . . ."

These were just some of the differences we encountered. It is easy for me to understand why Vivien, bilingual and born of Anglo parents, preferred to write in French, especially since I am also bilingual and can understand the nuances in both languages. Our purpose was to bridge this language gap in order to bring the woman and poet Renée Vivien to Anglo women who might not otherwise be able to read her.

Mostly we tried to bring to the experience of this project not only the skills of translation but also a sense of purpose born of captured imaginations and enraptured hearts.

A Personal Note:

Thinking of myself mostly as a political person does not prevent me from falling in love, obviously. Loving women, though, is still new to me, and while it is more appropriate to my politics than loving men, it is no less fraught with danger. Each experience is a drop in the tidal wave of undiscovered potential, and we realize that we are not in it just for ourselves. We watch and judge each other uncertain of how to proceed. As one well-aged yet still adolescent in loving women, my energy can be high-spirited and undisciplined; at times there seems to be no proper way to live it—too many blocks, distances, voids, and realities.

Enter Renée Vivien, and the activist turns to poetry. What one cannot express in life can be channeled into the word. Poetry gives joy, consoles and tempers the spirit.

Renée's unbridled expression of passion first attracted me; her vision moved me. I found within me the paradox she sharply drew: the envisioned communion of spirits ruled by desire, alongside the pain of an unyielding, unimaginative, and indifferent reality. Vivien was fascinated by death as perhaps a resolution of and release from such contradictions—an attitude one may disapprove of, yet understand. That her writing may have been for her a means of survival we can be grateful for.

Whatever personal framework you bring to Vivien's poetry, here is the intensity of a woman-identified-woman's experience that cannot leave one indifferent. And if you happen to be one who is magnetized by her as she was by shining Mytilene or by morbid Venetian waters, you are promised a privileged connection: never again will you look upon violets, lilies, opals, or evening in the same light.

—Bonnie

INTRODUCTION: THE EROTIC CONTINUUM

In place of a hermeneutics, we need an erotics of art.

–Susan Sontag

Who are we women to one another? The connection so close that the dead continue to speak to us, even haunt or direct us. In the months that I have worked on this translation, I have held Renée Vivien in my arms at times, and in some strange way she has been part of my own expiation. Some intermingling of time and space, an erotic continuum that joins our lives to each other–*erotic.* A word we ourselves shun from using, so powerful are the conventions, the male myths turned against us. To understand Vivien and our relationship to the whole feminine lineage, we must see eroticism not just in its limited sexual sense, but in a more expansive way that includes the full range of love. It is this expansive quality of eroticism that is at the base of our lives, and the interweaving of our lives and lines of poetry, and our myths and heritage. To see Renée Vivien with a clear eye is becoming more difficult as she becomes more known. In a relatively short time, she has gone from obscurity to an interest that often borders on cultism. She has something more lasting to offer, not only in the tradition of "Lesbiana" but, more importantly, in terms of the connection between our literature and our mythic power and how our awareness of that connection can be both healing and transmutative–part of the gifts of love we give to one another.

I don't think it was any accident that led me to read the *Big Mama Rag* article on Vivien, nor any accident that I am also a poet who was intrigued by her. She came to me at a time in my life when I was trying to take the "plunge inward" and when I was seeing the extent to which my emotions could be crippling and myopic. It was also at that time that I promised myself and whoever else in the cosmos was listening that I would go anywhere and do anything to be able to translate her and make her poetry more accessible to women. From that point on, the energy steadily mounted. The personal connection between us became a growing bond that defied the laws of matter.

On one level the energy was very pragmatic. When I had trouble finding a copy of the manuscript, I was "told" to take a trip, though at that time I didn't know where. At the last minute I decided on Denver, and there the last address leading me to the manuscript came. As I began the translating itself, I wondered where I would get it printed and if I would have to learn how to print. Two days later a woman offered to pay my tuition for a printing class.

Most dramatic was the way Bonnie came. I had just translated the poem "*L'amour borgne*"–one-eyed love. I see out of only one eye and realized as I was working that my ego could not tell if Vivien meant "one-eyed" literally, or metaphorically as "sly." References to eyes abound in her work, which includes one volume entitled *Venus of the Blind.* Energy began redistributing itself inside me. There were too many parallels for them to be coincidental. I needed an editor. I needed to understand what the link was between Vivien and me, and what we were helping each other purge that we hadn't been able to get rid of alone; I needed someone who could help me look at the text objectively. Several days after translating "*L'amour borgne*" Bonnie and I met in New Mexico. In the land of the *pénitentes* came a woman who spoke French and was a poet and was interested.

There were many small psychic things happening that defied accurate description. Still, why Vivien's connection to me? And why had this gifted, beautiful woman been so intent on flirting with death all her brief life? In my own life I had been trying to deal with the tendency toward sadness, trying to understand the part of me that is self-destructive, that punishes me with obsessive thinking, with a clinging to the past. I tried to do more than casually note that my Pisces moon indicated such tendencies (I wonder what Vivien's chart would reveal). I wanted to actively deal with "my shadow" and find a way out. In my case, I knew I didn't find madness attractive; it was only that certain behavior had become a vicious cycle, a closed circle rather than a spiral outward. I was in search of tools and inspiration, and they came to me from a dead sister. For in seeking what made Vivien "starve" herself to death, why she had been slowly killing herself over a period of years, I found the answers I was looking for.

The poems themselves offered the clues, and one by one they began sifting out the truth for me. In "*Sous la rafale*" ("Under the Storm") Vivien mentions a cry of horror that is found throughout her work. In another book, *Etudes et préludes*, she refers to "*quelque chose d'affreux qui pleure horriblement*" ("something awful that cries in the night"). Indeed, there was an incredible cry of anguish in Vivien that could never reach catharsis. In "*Sous la rafale*" she compares herself to Shakespeare's King Lear, who dove into madness until it brought him vision and release; and Dante, who made the descent into Hell only to return to Paradise. Lear had his ballast in Kent, who offered him love and solace. And the Fool poked handy-dandy at him, making him laugh in the face of it all, the saving laugh that might have pulled Vivien out of the gloom that she not only surrounded herself with but became enamored of. And what is more, Lear himself had the madness of Edgar, which, like that of the shaman in Indian culture, could guide him through his torment: madness raised to a cosmic and mythic level. And Dante also was not alone. There was Beatrice to guide him and the Catholic church to pronounce his journey into the depths as sacred. We make tragedies for Lears, epic cantos for the Dantes. They had the whole of the patriarchal path to walk on and substantiate them.

Vivien was truly out on some private heath, trapped in an emotional morass she could neither plunge into deeply enough to transform, nor see in some life-giving perspective, lacking as she did the models we have today with the Movement and with the benefit of history (her story and those of all the "sad" lesbians). She never saw herself in light of something other than the personal, the sick, her *maladie.*

One day near the end of translating, I reread Jeannette Foster's book *Sex Variant Women in Literature.* There, nestled in her chapter on Barney (Natalie Clifford Barney was Vivien's first love of passion; and their continuing liaison along with the undying love Vivien felt for Violet Shilleto, her childhood friend who died early and hauntingly, are the two key relationships in Vivien's life), was a quote from Proust that so unnerved me I left the library and my work and wandered into the streets, trying to assimilate the tears of joy and recognition. Proust had said, " . . . each individual follows repeatedly a compulsive emotional pattern, and does not profit by experience." In the same instant that I realized he was wrong, I decided he was also right. For him, for Vivien, perhaps for many of that time and even today, that was a psychological truth. That it had been for me and was no longer reflected how different I was at the end of this odyssey into Vivien from the way I had been at its beginning.

Translating is more than finding word equivalents in another language. For me, it was an opening of the curtains onto someone else's mind and life–which in turn unveiled my own. Breaking patterns is a long process, requiring many experiences over the years that allow us to observe ourselves and to bring the patterns from the unconscious to mindfulness. Did Vivien break her cycle through me? That may be impossible to answer;

but it is essential for us to ask why she never broke her pattern of melancholy while she was alive, to ask why her absorption with death and sadness consumed most of her life, became her lover ("I am able to love only what hurts me"). Her life was a tableau confusing the real and the fictional: she became a "Lesbia Brandon" (Swinburne's character), and Violet, and Sappho: in short, her sense of self was her own romantic conception of herself.

Joseph Campbell offers some insight here. In his book *Myths to Live by*, he explains the difference between essential schizophrenia and paranoid schizophrenia. The distinction is important in understanding Vivien's slow suicide over a period of eight years or more. Essential schizophrenia resembles the journey of a hero as portrayed in Western myth, an odyssey into self as well as countryside. This inner experience, accompanied by societal approval, parallels the journeys the shamans made, facing all the demons of the unconscious, mastering fears, sorting out the collective and personal unconscious, healing disintegration so that the return to rational consciousness restored not only the individual but the rest of the social group as well.

Most of us, Campbell asserts, merely project our demons outside, and they come back to haunt us. Instead of following the journey inward to fullest completion, we remain on the level of paranoid schizophrenia: we are not withdrawn from the world but remain ultra-sensitive to it, all the while fearing the worst from it, though the actual assault is from within.

And so it was with Vivien. She was a victim in her own field of projected unconsciousness. She never dealt fully with death or separation, though she felt their pain and its effect on her identity and ability to nourish herself. The pain she felt was probably given more import by her use of drugs and liquor. She became trapped in her own personal psychosis, as have many women—and as many continue to be. There was nothing or no one in her surroundings in the *belle époque* that could help, not that any of them lacked sympathy. There was no rite of passage for a woman at that time, much less for one who had chosen exile from family, country, and language. The very name *Renée Vivien* suggests that she hoped to be born anew, but she never escaped her patterns. That she was able to distill her anguish into poesy is not a feat to be underestimated. Hers was a society offering no guideposts for her—and consciousness is still a rare commodity.

She sought some sense of herself in the myths of Lesbos and the Greeks, on the one hand, and in the two great loves of her life, on the other—yet she never made the connection between public myths and private dreams. With the two great loves of her life, Vivien had touched a pulse of life within herself. But in one horrible year she lost them both, Violet to the grave, Barney to life.

Barney said she had wanted to bring sunshine and life into Vivien's world, to create an opening of light. Vivien needed to be drawn out, but she sought the solution to her sense of incompleteness through her lovers, hoping they might offer her some validation, some idea of who she was. That gesture is always doomed, always short-lived and futile, since it is only within ourselves that wholeness lies. Vivien had bought the Romantic myth "I complete you / you complete me." The true healing is a love affair with oneself. Women can share skin, can share processes with one another, but the unity we crave in sisterhood, in making love, is only possible if we bring to it a self already united and self-nourishing. As Barney or Violet could not hope to provide with their love or passion the validation Vivien craved, neither can we today view an erotic continuum in the way Vivien did. We do need the reemergence of a viable mythology, an ontology that would allow women to incorporate our private demons into the collective landscape to be purged. As it is, we splinter off into activists and ritualists, rather than bringing together our parts to form a practical, unified mythology.

It was perhaps in search of such a legitimizing mythology that Vivien returned to Sappho over and over again in her life and writings. Sappho was for her the legend of high rite, the imagery and puissance of nature, the feminine and real individualizing power. Sappho did after all incorporate her love for women into an actual, living community where the relationship between mortal love and goddess worship was real as well as ideal. The hope of such a unifying vision of love, the integration of mind and body, offered Vivien an alternative to her obsessions and to her love affair with death. It was a vision of life made attractive—so much so that Vivien and Barney actually set off for the isle of Lesbos, fully intending to set up another women's society in Mytilene. The plan was never realized, outwardly it appeared, because another woman brought Vivien back to Paris. Essentially, the plan failed because Vivien could not translate the world in her head into the world outside her.

That is why the landscapes in her poetry are so important, why an understanding of her choices of natural imagery, of her whole absorption with the symbolic use of nature, is necessary for an understanding of her life and work. It would be too facile merely to link her with the *symbolistes*, though of course she is a decadent at heart. However, like the *symbolistes*, she makes nature a correlative for her inner states. Her nature is no wasteland either; it is a verdant, lush, even lusty setting at times. At others, it is a mental landscape peopled and thinged by her fantasies and terrors. Above all, it is informed by the excessive emotion that she felt and could never quite release or express, although she did, after all, write thirteen books in approximately ten years before she died at thirty-two. Some brief comet. Some exquisite fire that she extinguished herself in over and over again, taking death, and not the phoenix, for her lover.

In some instances the relationship of natural image to person or time is clear: lilies are Barney; the violets, Violet; the roses usually are Sappho. Most of the time the exotic and erudite names she uses are precise in the mood they evoke. She delves into a microscopic world to try to correctly name the feeling and texture she wants to convey. Yet there never is an "objective correlative"–never an image or name or book or poem equal to her passion or the weight of her emotions. The landscape remains too cerebral. Vivien was a cultured woman of the city whose world never took on the feeling of real dirt between her fingers, and that was part of her tragedy. Barney absorbed the city background into her earthy, sensuous relationship with life. For Vivien, all out-there evoked her state of mind and her attachment to pain as somehow being the natural state of affairs for her. Her nature is not a wasteland in the sterile male sense, but neither is her nature life-giving or spiritual or ecological. She drowns in her own symbology, for when women are spiritually cut off from their roots–psychic and mythic–they are cosmically unecological. They can lay waste their bodies, cut down the bridge between the real and the unreal, or ideal–between the thing itself and the myth. The bridge between is often a symbol. In this context, Vivien is a *symboliste* gone awry. She could not jump the synapse, could never make the connection between her world of words and her pain and the way leading out. The symbols and referents began pointing inward rather than originating in nature. These are not flowers nor a landscape from nature. They are right out of her head. Our roots, to be sane and nourishing, must originate in nature.

For me Vivien's character is expressed in the Conrad Aiken story "Silent Snow, Secret Snow" where he speaks of the "flower that does not blossom out, but grows inward: it comes inward instead of opening . . . it is a flower becoming seed, life turned inward unto itself."

And we today, in search of our own roots, cannot help but feel some keen excitement in discovering this woman and others of the period. But we must see Vivien in some healthy perspective lest the madness and sadness seem only "period pieces." We are, I believe, creating our past at the same time as we are creating the present, and part of the burden of that discovery is a burden of love. With Vivien the sense of love is never consummated, as indeed her love was not consummated with Violet, nor with herself. Vivien's was a love that remained removed from the body. In many ways this woman starved herself of the essential nourishment.

There is no need to let madness become attractive nor to shy away from the mythic qualities of that brief period in Paris. The greatest gift of love we can give to ourselves and to Vivien is to see the relationships among our words, and our experience with nature, and our love, which is the essence of it all. To place Vivien in our arms with all the care of a lover. To heal the natural that is out of joint, to nurture the roots.

There is a vital sensuousness in Renée Vivien's work, a powerful eroticism, an unabashed giving of herself to both the moment and to her lovers—even to their memories, so that for her the past was also the present. And Vivien is part of our present as well as our past. We women are linked in an erotic continuum, a circle that spirals out into time and encompasses myth and love. Our awareness of our place in that circle is in itself both healing and devotional. Ours is the sweet sisterly hour of hand-in-hand.

—Sandia

Renée Vivien:

AT THE SWEET HOUR OF HAND-IN-HAND

The original edition of *A l'heure des mains jointes* bears this dedication:

"*A MON AMIE*

H. L. C. B."

And this quotation:

". . . the hour of sisterly sweet hand-in-hand."

—Dante Gabriel Rossetti

AT THE SWEET HOUR OF HAND-IN-HAND

I have childed my heart in the innocence
Of our love, awakening the enchanted chalice.
In the gardens where silence is accented,
Where the jaded laugh recovers its innocence,
O *chère*! I adore you with simplicity.

Your fingers fastened around my rough heart.
In a stammering like the naive cry
Of inexperience and gratitude,
I will tell you how, weary of the rough sea,
I have dropped anchor in the port where the skiff is moored.

Your hair, your voice, your arms have healed me.
I have cast off fear and brutal suspicion
I have shed the artificial and the bizarre . . .
I shelter my heart from a long sickness
Recovering slowly under your healing roof.

I have the security still somewhat shaky
Of one whose eyes, filled with images, are heavy,
And I rejoice at the grasses, and the plants;
I relax in blue noons, a little shaky
From having so long dreaded the aspect of bad days.

At the sweet sisterly hour of hand-in-hand,
I have contemplated, serene, a shadowy face,
Much like convalescents under clean linen,
The fever gone . . . at the hour of hand-in-hand,
I gave you the last lilies of my past.

SAPPHO LIVES AGAIN

The moon would rise in Lesbos in ancient times
Over the nocturnal orchards where lovers kept watch.
Love once satisfied ascended toward sleeping waters
And sobbed in the deep heart of sarbitos.

Sappho garlanded her face with august violets
And celebrated Eros who swept down like a wind
On the oaks . . . Atthis heard it while dreaming,
And the roses opened their warm, moist scent boxes.

The shores glisten, blond with the weight of the sun . . .
The virgins instruct beautiful strangers
How the shade is auspicious to their light caresses,
And the sky and the sea unfold their scenery.

Certain among us have conserved the rites
Of this shining Lesbos golden as an altar.
We know that love is powerful and cruel,
And our loves have the white feet of the Kharaties.

Our bodies are for their bodies a reflecting mirror.
Our companions, with breasts like spring snow,
Know in what strange and suave manner
Sappho once bent Atthis to her desire.

We women love with an infinite candor,
With the amazement of an astonished child
For whom a whole new world has opened up . . .
Sappho lives again now that we love as only women can.

We know how to brush with a kiss of velvet,
We know how to embrace with the pale heat of passion;
Our caresses are our melodious poems . . .
Our love is greater than all loves.

We repeat these words of Sappho, when we are
Dreaming under a sky illumined with silver:
"O *belles,* toward you my heart is never changing . . ."
Those that we love have spurned men.

Our lunar kisses have a pale sweetness,
Our fingers never offend the soft down of a cheek,
And we can, when the belt comes undone,
Be at once both lovers and sisters.

In us tenderness is stronger than passion
And yet the love of a child subdues us
According to the will of the harsh Aphrodite,
And each of us always remains her priestess.

Sappho lives again and reigns in our quivering bodies;
Like her we have heard the siren,
Like her, we have serene souls,
We who do not heed the insults of passersby.

Fervently we pray, "Let the night be doubled,
We whose kiss dreads the dawn,
We whose mortal Eros has unbound the knees,
We who are a flesh dazzled and troubled . . . "

Our lovers wouldn't know how to deceive us,
Since it is the infinite which we love in them . . .
And since their kisses render us eternal,
We who dread not the black oblivion of Hades.

Thus, we sing to them, with plain, sonorous soul.
Our days without shame, without fear or remorse,
Are unfolding in one great harmonious union,
And we love, like one loved in Mytilene.

LIKE THIS WOULD I SPEAK

If God bent his head askance at my death,
I would say to Him, "O Christ, I do not know you.

God, your strict law was never mine,
And I lived like a simple pagan.

See the sincerity of my poor, naked heart.
I do not know you. I have never known you at all.

I have slipped by like water, I was like sand.
If I have sinned, I was never responsible.

The world was all around me, like a garden.
I drank the clear dawn and crystalline night.

The sun girded me with vibrant flames,
And love inclined me toward the beauty of women.

The blue velvet sky spread out like a canopy . . .
A young virgin appeared on my doorstep. I was waiting.

Night fell . . . then the morning surprised us
Disagreeable, with its cloudy gray glimmers.

In my arms that pressed her close, she slept
As one sleeps in the arm of her lover.

Since then, I have lived in the turmoil of a dream,
All of eternity in that one brief moment.

She was beautiful, with her cold, bluish gray eyes,
And I loved this woman, in spite of your laws.

As I sought only for love, obsessed by a look,
The righteous people of this world have stoned me.

Those who were indignant at seeing my serene face
Hoped to bend me under the weight of their disdain.

But since I was born grievously proud,
I have scorned those who would throw stones at me.

And I listened only to the voice that I loved,
Having understood that no one else would ever understand . . .

Already the night approaches, and my perishable name
Is erased, like a word which one traces on the sand.

Sunset has burst forth like pressed wine . . .
No one will murmur my verses to the evening.

And now, Lord, judge me. For we are face to
Face, before the silence of men.

While it was sweet, love often treated me bitterly,
And I have earned neither heaven nor hell.

I would be a poor audience for your *cantique* of angels,
For having once heard strange chants.

The chants of Lesbos whose choruses have been silenced . . .
And I would hardly know how to celebrate your virtues.

I have never been given to wild revolt:
The kiss was the only blasphemy of my mouth.

Let me be, as I hurry toward the welcome evening,
Rejoining those who have never known you.

I will go far from your flock of chaste believers,
Remembering, along the paths of the wild daffodils,

And there, talking of love to the one that I see
So blond, who long charmed my ravished eyes.

I would learn that lilies are more lovely than roses,
And that song has less sense of infinity than the pauses . . .

Our eyes still filled with a sun long dead,
We will contemplate our burning past.

Sappho, her restless fingers on the sleeping lyre,
Will marvel at the beauty of my lover,

And the maiden of my desire, like the lily,
Will seem to her more graceful and supple than Atthis.

Sappho will shower us, in her fervent breath,
With the odes whose melodies charmed Mytilene.

And we will prepare the flowers and the flames,
We who have loved her in a century less beautiful.

Sappho will serve us, amid the gold and silk
Of soft cushions, nectar mixed with joy.

She will show us, in her graceful manner,
The Lesbian orchard that opens to the sea.

The sweet orchard, ringing with cicadas, where
The scent of the vine trails off, vibrant as a voice.

Our clothes undulate among the pale tunics . . .
Dika, Timas, Atthis, Eranna de Telos . . .

natalie Barney

We will see the bare breasts of a brown priestess
Who will lead a chorus dancing by the light of the moon . . .

O Christ, who one dreads at the hour of dying,
I have never known you at all. I do not know you.

I told you: I was a simple pagan.
Let me hasten toward the ancient sweetness,

And when finally the moment of my death arrives,
I will rejoin those who have never known you at all."

DRAW ME TO YOU, VENICE . . .

Without friend or book, wandering by the water's edge
That the sun beats down on, that the moon caresses,
Venice, I will be like a *Dogaresse*
Fascinated by the sleep of your dreary canals.

Ah, you know that sadnesses are overwhelming.
Since their will triumphs over instinct
And that only their face is striking and distinct,
Lure me, Venice, to the depths of your dead waters.

And say to those vulgar lovers of tomorrow
That I have judged them and feel contempt . . .
O you, solitary and haughty Venice!
Tell them that we laugh at their mortal happiness.

Disregard them: They are an insensitive lot
Those who taste no longer the precious ennui
Of being alone in the midst of mankind, people
For whom carnal disorder has killed conscious thought.

Tell them again, O you that weighs on the waters!
Mournful like me, and like me cold and somber,
Tell them again in my voice without echo, my voice of the shadow,
That death only is beautiful at the bottom of your canals.

WE WILL GO TO THE POETS

The shadows seem an enemy in ambush . . .
Come, I will carry you like a sick infant,
Like a plaintive child, sick and fearful.

I press your light body close between my nervous arms.
You will see that I know how to heal and protect,
And that my arms are strong, the better to protect you.

No more do the sacred woods have effective remedies,
And the world has always been cruel to women . . .
We know it . . . the world is cruel to women.

The censure of humans has weighed on our heads,
But we will go far away and forget them . . .
We have only to will it and we will forget them.

Remembering that there are vaster planets,
We will enter into the realm of the poets,
The marvelous realm where the poets sing.

The light moves there in a divine rhythm.
Enough of care: one can dream and finally be free . . .
Ma douceur, do you believe we can be free at last? . . .

I will build for you emerald palaces
Where perfume exudes, where music roves,
Similar to the memory that roves and lingers . . .

My love, which is raised to the level of a song,
Will praise your red hair more beautiful than sunset . . .
Ah! Your hair, more beautiful than the most beautiful sunset!

Eva Palmer

The pain will become exquisite and distant,
In the miracle of gardens and fountains,
The delicious gardens where the fountains rest.

Because I have trembled and cried like them,
Chère, I will go toward the luminous poets,
Without fearing the brilliance of their luminous faces.

I will say to them: "My work is an illusory work . . .
I walk obscurely toward a death without glory,
I am one who lives and will die without glory.

"But open up your ranks so jealously guarded,
Because I revered you once upon a time,
And I have read your verse once upon many an eve.

"Receive among you your sister without genius,
But whose soul is like your infinite soul . . .
Because my soul is so like your infinite soul.

"I find dawns sad and pleasure bitter:
Evening sees me wandering, watching the sea,
Feet bare, attentive to the refrains of the sea.

"Since desire has been my only poem,
Gaze upon the splendor of the woman I love . . .
O poets! See this woman I love!"

. . . We will enter, led by sister poets,
Into the land brought forth by their eternal lines,
Into harmony and moonlight eternal.

Night will reassure our anxious souls,
And we will watch the poets go by singing,
Grave and gentle, and the lovers of the poets.

WORDS TO MY FRIEND

Understand me: I am a mediocre being,
Not good, not very bad, peaceful, a bit cunning.
I detest heavy perfume and shrill voices,
And gray is more dear to me than scarlet or ocher.

I love the dying day which grows dim by degrees,
A fire, the cloistered intimacy of a room
Where the lamps, veiling their amber transparencies,
Redden the antique bronze and turn the gray stoneware blue.

My eyes drop to the carpet smoother than sand,
Indolently I evoke rivers flecked with gold
Where the clarity of the beautiful past still floats . . .
And nevertheless, I am quite guilty.

You see: I am at the age when a maiden gives her hand
To the man whom her weakness searches and dreads,
And I have not chosen a companion for the road,
Because you appeared at that turn in the road.

The hyacinth was bleeding on the red hills,
You were dreaming and Eros walked at your side . . .
I am woman, I have no right to beauty.
I had been condemned to masculine ugliness.

And I had the inexcusable audacity of wanting
Sisterly love fashioned with soft whiteness,
The furtive step that didn't trample the fern
And the sweet voice that comes to ally itself with evening.

They have forbidden me your hair, the look in your eyes,
It seems that your hair is long and full of odors
And it seems your eyes reveal strange longings
And grow agitated like rebellious waves.

They have pointed at me with irritated gestures,
Because my eyes searched out your tender look . . .
And seeing us go by, no one wanted to understand
That I had simply chosen you.

Consider the vile law that I transgress
And judge my love that knows nothing of evil,
As candid, as necessary and fatal
As the desire that joins lover to mistress.

They didn't read in my eyes how clearly I saw
The road where my destiny leads me,
And they have said: "Who is this damned woman
Who gnaws blindly at the flames of hell?"

Leave them to the concern of their impure morality,
And let us imagine that dawn has the blondness of honey,
That days without spite and nights without malice
Come, such as lovers whose goodness reassures . . .

We will go to see the clear stars on the mountains . . .
What matters to us, the judgment of men?
And what have we to doubt, since we are
Pure before life and since we love one another? . . .

MAY A WAVE CARRY IT AWAY

The tide, sleeping, prolongs a steady sigh,
The souls of shells float and whistle on the banks . . .
Everything is hostile to me, and my youth pains me.
I am weary of loving transient forms.
Upright, I take my heart where love was yesterday
So powerful, and look: I throw it to the sea.

May a wave light and dancing carry it off,
Let the sea make it party to its profound work
And carry it off at its pleasure like a dead thing,
May an inlet eddy suspend it to branches of coral,
May the will of contrary winds lift it up
And let it roll, among the pebbles on the beach.

May it falter and waver, one evening, trapped
By the long tresses of the blond algae,
May the dream of calm water be given to it
In the deceptive twilight of the waves . . .
And let my heart, subdued at last, tranquil and sweet,
Bend to the will of the wind and the current.

I throw it to the sea, like the rings of ancient rulers,
The rings of gold that the oblivious waves have tarnished,
And which fall, among the singing and the eulogies,
Into the transparent blue, into the infinite green . . .
The moment is vast, charming deaths are in her,
And I give my heart to the eternal sea.

LET'S GO INTO THE GARDEN

Ma douce, let us enter the abandoned garden,
In the primitive garden, exquisite and funereal,
Where the past likes to wander, solitary
And fierce, like an old dethroned king.

Let us enter in the garden overpowered by the autumn wind,
Where silence is beautiful like a woman in mourning,
Where the thorns of yesterday offer a hostile welcome
To her who bears not a single sweet regret.

In this garden where no one ever brings along
Her intrusive leisure and melancholy,
Among these lilies without freshness, that one forgets,
Let us hush, as in the distant time when I loved you . . .

The two of us, equally wearied, are seated
Under old walls rendered musty by old suns,
And having in us no longer the force of desire
Let us evoke the fragrance of past sadnesses.

Here young steps are taken indecisively . . .
The only ones harmonious, confident and suave,
Are the women who pass with the eyes of slaves,
Who love you still and whom you love no more.

Since here, the grass alone is wild and lively,
Let us linger and gather our memories.
Do you recapture golden days of long interludes,
The celebrations which you infused with your laugh of love?

See, the blue shadow gives a chambered effect.
A moth, wandering like a soul, alights
On your hair, prismed in blond, a bit green, a bit rose,
In the silence of the abandoned garden.

CONFESSIONS BEFORE THE EVENING

Ma très chère, I am happy now and calm,
My burning temples have been cooled by the dawn.

Come, I will tell you about my past, lay it bare . . .
And I will speak to you first of her hair.

Her hair framed her face in a virginal glow . . .
That kindness soothes pain she seemed not to know . . .

Her cold hair was more pale than a reflection of light,
And I had pursued her like an elusive swamp fire.

O, charm of my hours, surely you have guessed
You know, in fact, first loves are not the best . . .

That irritating kiss that gnawed at my flesh,
Corrosive as sea salt and more harsh.

Your dream echoes mine in the depths of my consciousness,
And not once was I calm or at ease in her presence.

She knew how to surround me with her arms, caress me,
But one day I knew this was not love, not really.

My long looks were never gratified by her grace.
I wanted more . . . yet one can tire of a face.

My daydreams resembled a flowerless spring.
"My eyes are dried up," I realized one evening.

Chère, I came to understand that her heart was double,
So clearly that thoughts of her gave me no trouble.

I no longer taste the bitter tears grown cold . . .
Look, the sun is brilliant as in pagan years of old.

Silence comes upon us leaving my mood nonchalant
And the moment slips away on the white feet of Atalanta.

The stream of summer moves like time, blue in its flow.
With a languorous happiness, I relax, I let go . . .

It seems I spoke deliriously before, lost my head . . .
Why don't we simply forget what I just said . . .

IN THE PUBLIC SQUARE

The floating clouds were unrolling their scarf,
In the clear sky, the color of wheat.
I was fervent and young, and I had my harp . . .
The world appeared, suave and feminine.

Grays of bark, greens of water, violets of the amaranth
Delighting my wide-open eyes . . . I heard
Laughing in me, from the depth of the past, the wandering
Soul and the musical heart of the Irish shepherds.

One morning, I followed some men and women
Who walked toward a town with blue roofs . . . I left
To follow them, the woods full of shadows and flames
And I carried my harp across the village.

Then I sang standing on the public square
Where the odor of dried fish drifted,
And, in the elation of my own music,
I didn't hear the noises of the market.

For I remembered that the very wise trees
Had talked to me, amid the silence of the woods . . .
Around me hissed the greedy bargaining
Mixed with the jeers of sly gossip.

In the crowd crying her bitter wares,
A woman saw me, offered me her hand,
And I thought for a moment she had understood me,
But the woman with bare arms went on her way.

I sang boldly—as the herdsmen sing—
Around me, the noise of the town ceased,
And as sunset cast its hearthlike glow
I saw that I was alone and the daylight was fading.

I set myself to singing without witness, for the joy
Of singing, like one does when love leaves you,
When hope mocks you and oblivion bruises you . . .
The harp shattered right in my hands in the night . . .

I LOVE YOU FOR BEING WEAK

I love you for being weak and coaxing in my arms
And for searching the sure refuge of my arms
Like a warm cradle where you can rest.

I love you for being red-haired like autumn,
Frail image of the Goddess of autumn
Lit up and crowned by the setting sun.

I love you for being slow and walking without a sound
And for talking softly and hating loud sounds,
As one does in the presence of night.

And I love you above all for being frail and faint,
And for moaning with frail sobs of dying,
In the cruel pleasure that persists and torments.

O sister of the Queens of yore, I love to see you,
Exiled in the midst of the splendors of yore,
Whiter than a reflection of moon on lilies.

I love you for not being alarmed, when ashen
And trembling I cannot hide my own ashen face,
O you that will never know how much I love you!

AFTER SWINBURNE

To Paule Riversdale

In remembrance of an epigraph of "The Double Being"

Can it be that I am cherished and desired,
Douce, since you alone are beautiful and not me?
I beg of you, with the fervor of my faith,
My arms laden with the flowers your smile accepts . . .

Yes, why am I beautiful in your eyes? And yet
Do not abandon me . . . if you want be free,
But keep for me this laugh where the soul floats and vibrates
This look, and this gesture half consenting . . .

Do not contemplate me, since you alone are beautiful.
Douce, don't love me, love my love
As impetuous and somber as that first day
When I was swallowed up in cruel ecstasy.

However, just once more, like yesterday,
Maîtresse, grant me the kiss of your mouth.
I will rejoice with you in a fierce
Nuptual cry, in a song of bitter triumph.

I will know how to be still, O most beautiful of faces!
I will not cry, if such is your wish.
We will walk in harmony toward evening,
More seřious in the middle of wise, sad mountains.

Living or dead, I will be reminded of you,
Of your lips, of the sharp design of your cheeks,
Of the movement sweet and slow with which you let down
Your hair, your neck, and your breasts rising in emotion.

If you want, squander with others other hours,
Ma maîtresse! But keep this hour for me,
Blossomed out like a pomegranate, like a rose,
When you brush it lightly with your breath.

It is sweet, for a little while, before death,
O *chère!* To tremble, to hope, to fear,
It is sweet, having drunk the ecstasy, to extinguish
Myself slowly, in autumnal agreement.

I KNOW A POND

> There is, in the heart of a valley, a pond called The Mysterious Pond.

I know a pond that dozes, turned wan
By the friendly moon and clear light of dawn.

An iris flourishes there, hardly like a lance,
And the dream of the water marries the silence.

Nothing breathes nor rustles the reeds.
The reflected sky mirrors the color of the seas.

Waves conceal a long regret wanton and tender,
And the silence waits with the troubled water.

There, the large water lilies lift their milky blooms,
The golden mayflies die there, two by two . . .

I will choose for you, words of praises
That run like water among the wild grasses.

The lilies offer their blue cups to the day above:
It is the raising of the chalices of love.

The mayflies, turning in couples, make one imagine,
Undulating and supple, pairs of waltzing women.

The lethean lotuses lift their pale faces . . .
My Loreley, let's glide slowly toward forgetfulness.

In a loyal farewell, let's stay intertwined
And let us die, like the weary dragonflies.

I will say to you: "Here is a pond mysterious
Which curious men will never experience.

Come to sleep amid the water lilies . . . the iris flutter,
And we embrace each other, we that die together . . ."

. . . I know a pond that dozes, turned wan
By the friendly moon and clear light of dawn.

And, under the water of the pond, that covets mysteries,
Two women are going to die there, like the mayflies . . .

LANDING AT MYTILENE

From the depths of my past, I return to you,
Mytilene, crossing the disparate centuries,
Bringing you my passion, my youth and my faith,
And my love, like a present of aromatics . . .
Mytilene, crossing the disparate centuries,
From the depth of my past, I return to you.

I rediscover your waves, your olive trees, your vines,
And your blue where I melt myself and am dissolved,
Your ships, and your mountains with their noble lines,
Your cicadas with their exasperated and crazy cries . . .
Under your blue skies, where I melt away and dissolve,
I recover your waves, your olive trees, and your vines.

Receive in your orchard a feminine couple,
Island melodious and auspicious to caresses . . .
Amidst the Asian odor of heavy jasmine,
You have not forgotten Sappho nor her mistresses . . .
Isle melodious and favorable to caresses,
Receive in your orchards a feminine couple . . .

Lesbos of the golden flanks, give us back our ancient soul . . .
Revive for us the lyres and voices,
The laughs of old, and the music of old
That rendered so poignant the kisses of long ago . . .
You that safeguard the echo of lyres and voices,
Lesbos of the golden flanks! Give us back our stolen soul . . .

Conjure up the tunics swaying in the night,
The blond and red glimmers of hair,
The gold cup and the necklaces and the mirror,
And the hyacinth flower and the faint murmurs . . .
Summon up the brightness of beautiful hair
And the filmy tunics which pass in the night . . .

When, laying out their bodies on beds of dried seaweed,
The lovers let fall their tired and weary words,
You mingled your odors with roses and peaches
To the long whisperings that follow the kisses . . .
In our turn, letting fall the tired, wearisome words,
We recline our bodies on your beds of dried seaweed . . .

Mytilene, ornament and splendor of the sea,
Like her versatile and eternal,
Be the altar today of the raptures of yesterday . . .
Since Sappho then with an Immortal one lay
Welcome us in the name of her love and in goodwill,
Mytilene, ornament and splendor of the sea.

MY FRIEND THE WIND . . .

I love you and salute you, friend wind,
Who prowls across the fields rich with planting,
And who comes leaning over the sea, drinking
The waves whose tartness freshens your pale thirst.

Nothing would know how to fill the emptiness of my arms,
And my impotent days have an unpleasant torpor . . .
I aspire to the infinite that one no longer acquires . . .
When will you carry me toward the rugged cliffs?

When will you carry me toward the gray horizons,
Toward the reefs and desolated islands
Where the plants have no magical poisons
That seek in vain the exiled princesses? . . .

When will you carry me toward eternal winter
Where no flight of white gulls ascends,
Where the nights have frozen the torment of the sea,
Where nothing human lives in the midst of the silence?

MY VICTORIES

I

As a triumphant arch filled with ochers and azure,
The horizons of night are opened large and pure.

When will I pass with my victories realized in my soul,
Under the arch erected for those who are acclaimed?

The memorable and vast arch encloses the sunset
And its curve seems like the proud rhythm of a song.

When will I pass, having on me the noise of wings
Created, in the sacred air, by my faithful Victories?

Of course, the hour is not for poets–and me,
I have only my youth, my force and my faith,

The triumphant arch is there clear among black nights.
When will I pass, under the wings of my victories?

II

I know it—today it does not hurt so much—
I will not pass under the triumphant arch.

And I will not hear the rapturous voices of women
Who sob, "Here is the gift of our souls . . ."

I will pass, without flowers, without laurels, without hope,
No one will wait for me, in the purple deep of night.

Resigned, and dwelling on the defeats of the past,
I will have on me, the noise of their weary wings . . .

Like an arch of triumph, filled with ochers and azure,
The horizons of night are opened, large and pure . . .

WHERE THEN WILL I GO? . . .

No movement of the waters, nor swaying of the boughs . . .
The gray becomes more gray, the night a deeper black,
And the song of birds cannot equal the silence . . .
Where then can I go, with my heart, this beautiful evening?

In the sky with its triumphant sunset, the clouds
Roll by, heavy and golden like chariots . . .
I am weary of the days, tired of voices and faces
And the repressed tears and noiseless sobs . . .

You who with your resemblance to royal lovers,
Relive at my side the faded joys . . .
To the future charged with feverish roses
I prefer the purple and gold of times past . . .

Let us go slow, among things too hasty . . .
One must not search . . . one must not desire . . .
Let's go with the full tide, without returning to shore . . .
Will you follow me, toward infinity, this beautiful evening? . . .

WEARY REFRAIN

The perfumes of the cytisus have softened the breeze
And one is saddened, wandering under the transparent sky . . .
The sun agonizes . . . and here the exquisite hour . . .
In the fragrant evening, one lingers, crying . . .

You return, frail and red-haired, O *ma belle!* O *ma douce!*
As if in a dream, I see your eyes distant and cold,
Like water without a ripple where regret is deadened . . .
Under their look, I feel I am reliving the past.

Dear shadow! I myself have shattered my poem . . .
I must not see you anymore, in the calm of evening . . .
Look at my pale face and feel how much I love you . . .
The darkness, sweet black veil, covers my despair . . .

An inexpressible rose has blossomed in the sand,
And while round about me the beautiful day fades
I will cry, as those whom the hour overwhelms:
"Nothing leaves no going back like impatient love . . ."

TO MY BELOVED

You are my palace, my evening, and my autumn,
And my silken sail and my garden of lilies,
My golden perfume vial and my white column,
My park and my pond of reeds and irises.

You are my perfumes of amber and honey, my palm,
My greenery, the song of crickets in the air,
My snow that is dying from being haughty and calm,
And my seaweed and my salty atmosphere.

And you are my bell with the weeping monotone,
My fresh island and my saving oasis . . .
You are my palace, my evening, and my autumn,
And my silken sail and my garden of lilies.

I WOULD GIVE MY EYES . . .

The world illumines the prisms of the poem . . .
I would give my eyes to my beloved woman.

Her dress, like silken winds, will rustle and sigh . . .
Humble and tender, I will say: "Here are my eyes . . .

I will give my eyes that have seen so many objects,
So many seas, so many roses, so many sunsets.

My marvelous eyes which once were posed
On the waters of the Bosphorus and the Eleusinian stones.

I've seen Seville where laughs the spirit of the courtesan,
Jerusalem and Smyrna with its caravans.

I've seen Granada yearning in vain for better times,
Where the nightingale loves and sings best her rhymes;

Venice, stretched out like a dying *Dogaresse,*
And Florence who had been Dante's mistress . . .

I've seen Hellene where the echo of Pan's pipe plays,
Egypt, with her immobile Sphinx's gaze.

And I've seen, near the waves that night makes serene,
Heavy with grapes, the lovely orchards of Mytilene.

I've seen Persia, her temples thick with scent,
Yedo, ringing with young girls' fragile chants.

Taken with the climates, the currents and the spaces,
Chère, I have seen China with her yellow faces . . .

I've seen the golden isles where the sweet air cools,
And the Hindu temples near their sacred pools.

The temples where survives the inscrutable wisdom . . .
I give you all that I have seen, my cherished one . . .

I return, bringing you my gray or joyous skies
And my far-aways–Accept the gift of my eyes."

WITHOUT FLOWERS AROUND YOUR HEAD

You didn't want to hear me . . . But what does it matter?
You whose virtuous anger was inflamed
At the moment I dared come knocking at your door,
You will never gather the roses of Sappho.

You will never see the gardens and riverbanks
Where the powerful harmony of her *paktis* sounds,
And you will not hear the sacred choir of virgins
Nor the hymn of Eranna nor the weeping of Atthis.

As for me, I have sung . . . No echo is awakened
In your house with walls warmly sleeping.
I am going away without anger or hatred, like
One who has no parents or friends.

I am not of those whom the crowd praises,
But one who is hated . . . Because I dared to imagine
That a virgin in love is more beautiful than a man,
And I have sought women's eyes in the heart of evening.

O my songs! We will feel neither shame nor sadness
When we taste scorn from those whom we scorn . . .
And it is no longer to the crowds that I address myself . . .
I have never understood the laws nor the reasons . . .

Let's go away, me and my disdainful songs . . .
What matters to us those who haven't listened?
Let us go toward the silence and shade that I love,
And let oblivion keep us in her eternity . . .

UNDER THE STORM

From the chaotic night a cry of horror is exhaled.
Come, we will wander, all three, under the storm . . .

The abyss cracks against us its black summons,
We will get through, O my eternal companions!

The lightning terrifies us and the night leaves us desolate . . .
O old Lear, like you I am lost and crazy.

And those of my family and those of my friends
Have spurned me with their wretched outrage.

Like you, Dante, overcome with a haughty pain,
I am the exile whose heart bursts with hate.

In spite of thunder and cold and wind,
No one has opened for me the doors of sanctuary . . .

My father, the mad king, my brother, the poet,
Look at my eyes and disheveled hair.

The peasants on the land, catching sight of the three of us
Cross themselves with an unconscious fear.

In spite of my hands without scepter and my head without crown,
I resemble you O Lear whom the world abandons!

In spite of the poverty of my obscure destiny
And my verse, I resemble you, O Florentine!

Listen to the thunder in the noise of the cymbals . . .
We will wander until dawn under the raging storm.

I CRY OVER YOU

The night closed in again, like a somber door,
On my ecstasy, on my transports of yesterday . . .
I evoke you, O splendid one, O daughter of the sea!
I come to weep for you, like one mourns a death.

The air of blue horizons no longer swells your breasts,
And your lifeless fingers are heavy with rings.
Was that not you who rode the crest of the waves,
Who now sleeps in the ease of cushions?

The storm and the infinite that once charmed you
Were they not perfect, were they not worth
The conjugal calm of hearth and table
And the security found in a common husband?

Your eyes have learned the art of that warm, empty look,
And the submissiveness of the lowered eyelid.
I see you, pining away in your apartment,
The painted lashes, the eyelids enlarged by kohl.

Your laziness and lifeless spirit
Have enchanted the dense dream and the leisure of
The man who taught you dull pleasure,
O you that yesterday had been the sister of the Valkyries!

Your husband shows your eyes today, once so
Contemptuous, your hands, your indifferent swan's neck,
Like one shows off his wheatfields, his garden, his vineyards,
To the admiration of self-satisfied friends.

Abdicate your kingdom and be the weak spouse
Without will before the desire of your husband . . .
Deliver your fluid body to the many currents,
Be more docile still to his jealous ardor.

Keep this paltry love that cannot deceive
Your spirit formerly possessed by dreams . . .
But never take back the rugged way of the shore,
Where the seaweed has the slow rhythm of a eulogy.

Hear no more the voice of the sea, heard
As in a dream across the night winged with gold . . .
For the night and the sea would talk to you still
Of your virginity, glorious and now lost.

MORNING GARDEN

Come, the hours of love are furtive and rare . . .
The morning garden is full of birds from afar.

Chère, I invite you to this feast royally adorned.
This morning I do not want to be pleasured alone.

Dawn strikes the sky like a door enclosed.
Come drink the dew in the heart of the rose.

Drink the dew like a liqueur fresh and tart.
My heart is a rose and I offer you my heart.

The dawn has the tint of abalone and mother of pearl.
Joy is simple and nothing is as beautiful as the merle.

Let's savor this ardor, somewhat sad, and we will cry
From feeling on our faces the day's first light.

Come, *ma très chère* . . . To the east the painted sky is changing key,
And the grass is sweet to the bare feet like a silk tapestry.

Without undue concern for hostile destiny,
Let's thank the morning sky in its mercy.

TO AN IMPOVERISHED GOD

I adore you, god poor among the immortals,
And I have woven for you these purple roses,
Because you have no temples or altars,
And no incense caresses your nostrils.

No one dreads you nor seeks your benevolence . . .
Those that honor you are poor, for you give them,
Having opened your hands wide, poverty;
And your breath is colder than that of autumn.

I who suffer the insults and outrage of the strong,
I bring to you, poor and sad god, these offerings:
Some violets that I gathered from the graveyard
And some tobacco blossoms that open, this wide . . .

In a chest of jade with a crystal clasp,
Simple god, I humbly bring you my dark heart,
For I am able to love only what hurts me,
In love with a phantom and the shadow of a ghost . . .

I ask nothing of your divinity
Without perfume, that no priest has recognized . . .
Nor no king has ever feared to have irritated you
And hasn't cried before your cold and bare shrine.

But I who hate those who crowd around the altars,
I who scoff at the greedy hope of prayers,
I dedicate to you, O sweetest of immortals,
This pious chant which flowers on my bitter lips.

EMINE

The sunset will cover the snow with opals,
And the air will be charged with scents oriental.

The secretive skiffs will throw out their lights
Like Argentinian fish that cross the sea at night.

It will be the risk that one loves and one doubts . . .
In slow steps, my destiny will march along the route.

Among the unknowns it will be recognized
In spite of changing skies and unexpected times . . .

My heart will beat like a flame vibrates . . .
While my destiny will be shaped by a woman who waits,

And my destiny will have hairs of deepest blue . . .
It will be the fantastic and miraculous come true.

Involuntarily, as when one tremors,
I will repeat to myself, "Every woman has her hour.

No other hour will be its peer
No one else will await, what I wait here.

She who will shine in the shadow solitary
Will lead me toward the domain of mystery.

At her side, I will enter, as pale as Aladdin,
Into a prestigious and terrible garden.

My dear destiny, with its slow movements,
Will pick for me the fruits of precious gems.

I will pass, amidst the fairyland bold,
Impassive before trees with trunks of gold.

And I will turn my back on the moon and the sun
And the asters in flower, for this dark-haired woman.

Her eyes will be the abyss into which falls the universe
And her hair will be the night where I am immersed.

At her bare feet, crying with infinite ecstasies,
I will let fall the lamp of genies . . .

ONE-EYED LOVE

I love you with my single eye, I leer at you
Like a Chinese at opium:
I love you with my one-eyed love,
Young girl as white as arum.
I want your dark brown eyelids,
And your voice slower than a timbrel;
I love you with my sinister eye
Where shines the anger of rum.

I follow you with my stare, like a wanton ape,
Drunk like a balloon without ballast.
Your fickle soul of a Sphinx
Floats between middling nonsense.
And I pant toward the bait
Of vibrant breasts, of supple torso
Where grace marries force,
And of eyes green like the west.

Your face is blurred across the curtains;
And you meditate, a dry fruit
Between your Florentine lips
Where a Greek smile is appeased.
I die at your brief words . . .
I want you with your teeth
To pierce my eye where dreams boil over
Like a macaw, with one sharp peck.

THEY CRY TOWARD EVENING . . .

The garden and the calm and the deepening light,
And all my memories that cry toward evening . . .
The sweetness of being alone and sad and just sitting
In the shadow, of no longer smiling and being weary . . .

The timeworn sighs prowl among the ferns,
And happiness itself is uncertain and trembles.
I am one who meditates and gathers up
My memories, my memories, my memories . . .

They glide like furtive ghosts,
With empty hands and deadened eyes, in some meadow
Without smells, and that no springtime has dappled.
Their step leaves no imprint on the shores.

They can no longer contain their suffocating sobs.
For some, with eyes dulled like old metal blades,
Cry behind veils like women cry;
Others cry without shame like children.

I am alone, I am no longer anyone's lover,
And I no longer adore a haloed smile
By sunset's rays: I look for myself in my past,
And I evoke the time when I was less at peace.

. . . Lighter than a bird, more frail than a rattle,
Here are the distant memories of my infancy.
They run away, their ribbons fly the color of hope,
Their skirts still smell of the essence of sachet.

And now, here are my mournful memories.
They pass, disdaining the dream and the effort
And crowned with the violets of death;
Their mourning clothes blend with the gloom.

I dream without ardor, like a pale recluse . . .
The Loreley that I have cruelly loved
Vanishes like a blond haze
And I feel today that I no longer love her.

Then, a memory laughs, and its laugh quavers . . .
–This laugh of an old woman where gaiety is cracked!
In the garden that bathes in a saddened silence,
The green shade deepens to the size of a cave.

I no more have the fervor, no more the desires,
I want only the peace of the garden and this hour . . .
It seems to me that yesterday I was a little better . . .
Leave me alone to cry with my memories . . .

VIVIANE

A fresh smell, sounds of hushed music play
Under the leaves, and it is Viviane the fay.

She imitates from behind a mass of flowers,
The bantering laugh of birds high in the bowers.

Sovereign of fantasy, she lingers and prowls
In the forest, as in emerald palace halls.

The water mirrors the color of her face.
Around herself she wraps the mist, veil of lace.

Sometimes, a languor arises from the grass like a fan:
The violets have all greeted Viviane.

Her dress moves with pearl and silver softly gleaming,
Her face is variable and her heart always changing.

Her feminine power insinuates itself in the twilight:
She becomes irresistible by pale moonlight.

Some shepherds believe to have seen, in their innocence,
Gliding along her bare arms, green serpents.

At midnight the fairest star crowns her head;
Sometimes she is cruel; sometimes she is good.

More powerful than fate is Viviane;
She carries sleep and death in her hand.

More than hope, more than dream, she is fair.
The great enchantresses are children next to her.

In her arms, memory is an abolished dream.
Her magic kiss is colder than oblivion.

Her hair is let down and the sun turns it blond.
Each morning she is more golden than the dawn.

Undulating, she knows how to promise and deceive.
Toward sunset, her hair becomes red as the eve.

At the vague hour where regret is concealed,
Her distant eyes with twilight gray are revealed.

When the ambered thread of crescent trembles in light
Under the oaks, she turns brown dusk like the night.

Kings have shared her golden bed and her table's grace,
But to none has she ever shown her true face.

She is born anew, grows each day in beauty,
And her illusions beguile the simple love's purity.

She wanders, like an April wind, under the greenwood,
And you see in her your love, the prize of maidenhood.

She is the one whom we meet only once.
Listen . . . No voice is like her voice.

She approaches, her fingers pulling petals from the buds.
You tremble . . . You have forgotten the words . . .

But you know–the magic wood has chanted it–
That she has belonged to you since all eternity.

She has changed her name, her voice, her visage;
In spite of all, you recognized her in passage.

She awakens in you all the ancient desiring.
In the shadow of her steps shines remembering.

You had presentiments of her, and you had dreamed of her
At great length, and above all you have recovered her.

She weaves for you skies and gardens,
You fall asleep in her eternal arms.

SHE PASSES

The sky frames her like a shrine,
And I would live one hundred years without seeing her again.
She is the sudden: she is the miracle of evening.
The religious moment blazes and tolls . . . she passes . . .

I came with the throng of lepers,
But, since dawn, I knew I would be cured.
They look to her with idolatry
And cry in soft voices . . . And I cry with them.

Her vesperal look illuminates the space
And her bare feet have sanctified the road.
A mysterious lily has fallen from her hand.
The sobs are stifled quickly . . . she passes . . .

Of all us who were crying, she has made her choice . . .
A bell is set in motion and the world listens . . .
She will no longer return this way,
But I see her pass and I no longer suffer.

We imagine that our spirit will be more weary,
And that our fear will be more intense and more bleak
When her dress will have disappeared in the night.
But we will have known the miracle . . . she passes . . .

TWILIGHT HAPPINESS

Your dark rings of amethyst
Animate and tremble slightly
By the yellow glow of the fire . . .
Outside the light persists.

Let us welcome the dream, giver
Of enchantments and fairylands . . .
Let us mingle our tempered souls
And talk of our happiness.

Let us talk of gladness, *ma très chère,*
Like one talks of a friend,
Picturing in the sleepy fireplace,
Her familiar resemblance.

Everything conspires to help us
In an eager complicity . . .
Let's whisper: "My tranquil soul
No longer dreams of the future."

Joy becomes easier to understand
With the intimacies of winter,
When the spirit of a tender twilight
Floats and whispers in the air.

Happiness is woven with forgetfulness;
It does not know about hope;
It resembles the deliverance
After a labor finally accomplished.

And joy is to be sitting here
With you, round the hearth,
And to see the fire redden
In your calm gray eyes.

It is to silence the vain confessions
And to forget the other women,
While watching the flames gleam
Across the fullness of your hair.

It is seeing autumn catch flame
In the fire's shifting lights,
Where all the towers and palaces
Facades and columns crumble and fall . . .

In my heart which shivers a little,
A sob from another time is caught . . .
See how happiness can be sad,
Winter evenings around the fire . . .

SPANISH PENITENTES

Visionary repentance no longer wears out their knees.
Among the blighted fields and sick towns
They dance, like black bacchantes.
Sometimes the night wind extinguishes their candles.

They have cut off their long, proud hair:
The hair shirts have lacerated their tender breasts,
Their psalms, whispered or uttered in large cries,
Are accompanied by the grating sound of bells.

Meanwhile, asleep in the depth of their Spanish eyes
Are memories that are like a Moorish garden
Where the fountain retraces a white arabesque,
Where the voices of a thousand nightingales are exhalted.

And it is in vain that these wanton *pénitentes*
Publicly call out their clamors of remorse . . .
Until day when worms will gnaw their dead eyes,
Their flesh will not forget its consenting weakness.

Their bruised flanks are already in a swoon,
And their mouths of passion open their warm red,
For the winds of Granada and the winds of Toledo
Blend their heavy perfumes with the noise of prayer.

They will not see, with their feverish eyes,
Heaven where one no longer keeps memories of love,
From where, cold in its whiteness, the eternity of day
Banishes the voluptuousness with its dark passion.

They will not enter the limpid clear sky,
But, in the burning night where weep the damned,
Love, regenerated from the tombs of the years,
Will be alive to lighten their torments in hell.

IN THE HARBOR

Weary like the waves, weary like the sails,
I enter the port filled with spindrift and stars.

I had fled the clear country and pleasant climates
To sleep in this harbor where the sails take rest.

I have lost the desire for savage liberties,
And I no longer know the thirst for long voyages.

So many golden dreams find a way to deceive you,
That one comes to feel less youthful toward evening.

In vain, I have followed the coasts of charming lands
That have betrayed me, much as a lover can.

I hoped to find there fruits of rubies and blue gold,
Rivers of deep red garnet and roses of fire.

But I learned that a banal sun shone down on them,
And that misleading distance made them seem beautiful.

Here, I will find a nocturnal peace . . . here,
The shadows are tinged with soft violet . . .

And, in this harbor, where the stars are reflected,
I will see other sails set forth without regret.

THE INSATIABLE THIRST

Yesterday I was a solitary voyager.
I went, carrying in my heart a bitter anxiety . . .
I needed you like a wave of summer,
Like a purifying wave where one is refreshed.

Today, my silence has some thoughtful joys.
O *très chère!* and my soul is a full cup,
The world is fresh as an orchard in Mytilene:
I no longer dread the evening that weeps under the yews.

I had need of you like of running water
That one hears and that cradles your sorrow
With a musical and serene rustling . . .
I heard your clear voice like water that sings.

Your voice was flowing, at once both murmur and cadence,
Chère, and my soul was steeped in deepest blue,
And I felt then my quiet sorrow
Melting . . . I heard the pure water of your voice.

Since then, the weight of white noons enchants me,
And my thirst no longer dreads the irritating sun . . .
I had need of you like a wave of summer,
I had need of you like water that sings.

I WAS A PAGE IN LOVE

It is the hour when desire implores and persuades . . .
The world is in love like a serenade,
The night air breathes the languors of a serenade.

The workers of night, your magical friends,
Have woven with gold your robe of silk
And seeded with blue iris the weave of the silk.

It seems as though we come one to the other
From some deep unknown past that was ours,
From a stately and tragic past that was ours.

On my lips a charming memory lingers.
Who can know? I was perhaps your lover . . .
O *ma splendeur!* I was once your lover . . .

A shadow of sadness a bit cruel persists,
Drawing thinner yet your Florentine mouth . . .
Ah! the piercing smile of your Florentine mouth!

My remembrances are more tenacious than a hope . . .
The soul of a page in love lives in me tonight,
A page who sang beneath your balcony at night . . .

THE PALM TREE

At my awakening, was the miracle of the world,
The dreamy blue sky and the waves of vibrant gold,
The Mediterranean . . . And I began to dream,
So wise and profound was the peace of dawn,
That for us alone the universe was alive,
And we were the soul and center of the world.

Lost in the furthest part of the garden this morning,
From the tree I broke off for you this palm
That the earth nourished with sap strong and calm.
Over there, where the clear air is a crystal vibrating,
Très chère, you will take in your hands the branch of this palm
That I have broken off, in the mystery of the morning.

But I have chosen, to frame you, O *la plus belle!*
The voluptuousness of this Italian decor,
Of this sky whose laugh is less sweet than yours,
Of this sea who sees the moon emerge from her . . .
See, the prestigious Italian decor
Alone is worthy of framing you, O *la plus belle!*

And you, knowing that nothing triumphs over beauty,
Neither power, nor faith, nor genius,
You smile, victorious, unknowable, infinite,
Perfect in your sweetness as in your cruelty,
Greater than the proudest efforts of genius,
O pale woman in whose being triumphs beauty!

GARDEN OF DARKNESS

The hours have cooled the fire in my bones,
And their heavy gloom has weighed on my head . . .
Now the too clear distances will mellow
And the night will open for me its garden of gloom.

Solitary, while the time runs along and escapes,
I will gather the flowers of regret and dreams.
Grateful for the sweet charm that stays awhile,
I will offer the perfume of my soul to the night.

The poems have lines far too regular,
The music, a sound too clear, too transparent . . .
I will knock soon at the doors of the garden
Which will open for me, large and familiar.

For the night loves me: she has known that I loved her . . .
And, knowing that I am resigned and withdrawn,
She carries for me, as in an ebony coffin,
The sadness of times past and never . . .

Night will entrust to me the black lily and rose
And its violets of darkest blue,
And I will linger in the corner of its walls
That seem like those of cities royally enclosed . . .

Little matters to me today the caprice of fate . . .
Night is opening for me like the garden of a queen
Where I will parade my serene sensuality
And my indifference with regard to death.

WE WERE SEATED

Ma douce, we were like two exiled spirits,
And we carried in us our desolate hearts.

The air of dawn throbbed, painful as a disease . . .
No one knew how to talk in our native speech . . .

While we wandered among people and strangeness,
The morning smells had lost their light essence.

. . . When you rose up, like a hope, above me,
Your sad dress was the color of the evening.

Watching the night fall, we took these seats,
To feel the pleasant freshness of the breeze.

Since we were no longer alone in the universe,
We tasted with more leisure the beautiful verses.

Chère, we hesitated, without daring to believe again,
And I said to you: "Evening is more beautiful than dawn."

You gave me your face, you gave me your hands,
I no longer feared the tomorrows, the uncertain.

The colors extinguished their splendid insolence;
No voice came to interrupt our silence.

I forgot the houses and their refusal to welcome us . . .
The sunset tinged with sandia my mourning clothes.

And I said to you, touching your eyelids half-closed:
"The violet is more beautiful than the rose."

Shadows overtook the horizon, like water rising . . .
And all around us the harmonious sob of life welling . . .

A languor drowned out the city powerful and rude,
We savored fully the hour in its plenitude.

Slow death gently effaced the noises and the light . . .
I came to know the august face of night.

And you let glide at your bare feet your veils . . .
Your body appeared to me, more noble under stars.

This was the repose, the return, the appeasement . . .
And I said to you: "Here is love's fulfillment . . ."

Once, carrying our desolate hearts in us,
Ma douce, we were like two exiled spirits.

DEPARTING

The lamp of long evenings throws a ray of amber
On the picture frames, toning down the antique golds.
The hour of my departure has chimed in the next chamber . . .
The night is black and I can see nothing outside.

I no longer recognize the face of things
That were the witness of good days and bad . . .
Now, even the familiar scent of roses is dying . . .
The night is black, and I don't know where I am going.

Should I regret . . . perhaps . . . this time past . . .
But I am not owned by needless regrets . . .
I walk straight ahead, the future is my master,
And, whatever my lot, I will no longer return.

THE LIE OF EVENING

Well, by one such evening, I believed I was a poet . . .
I had dreamed, in the too exquisite silence,
Of suns possessed and laurels conquered . . .
And my life feels like the day after a celebration.

Everything hurts me, summer, the ray of the beacon
Red on the night water, and the rhythm of oars,
Rosebushes in a garden and the long hair of women
And their looks. Everything hurts me, everything hurts.

Come to me, my two loves, my beloved ones . . .
I will surround you with your decor of old,
I will return your flowers, your gems, your gold,
And I will rekindle your burned-out torches.

You were my splendor, my glory and my song,
You, Loreley, light of moon, laugh of opal,
And you whose presence is calm and vesperal,
And whose love is more pensive than the setting sun.

You, the one that my desires and tears have adorned,
The one that I loved yesterday, the one I love today,
Let us find palaces from where the queens have run away,
And find the weakened seas that have no tide.

The last shiver of gold is silences in the hornet's nest . . .
You, pale like Atthis, and you, girdled with roses
Like Dika, let's march together on the sullen roads
That did not know how to keep the imprint of our feet.

The despotic present is like a rude master
Tormenting the slave whose sleep is harrassed . . .
Mes chères, let us descend the slope of the past
Feeling the evenings full of lassitude.

I muse on the fatigue, the ennui of returns
Which follow the departures toward charming lands . . .
Let us go into the future, O *mes amantes!*
Knowing that we have lived our most beautiful days.

TOWARD LESBOS

You will come, your eyes full of night and of yesterday . . .
And it will be by a beautiful sunset on the bay.

Frail like a cradle on the smooth waves rises,
Our ship will be laden with amber and spices.

The winds will submit, convinced of my right.
I will inform you, "The sea is ours tonight."

Your fingers will resemble the long fingers of the drowned.
We'll go forth at random, with full sails we'll be crowned.

You will ask me, eyes filled with wonder and charms,
"On what unknown bed will I sleep in your arms?"

The birds will sing, hidden in the sails.
We will watch stars appear, the first most pale.

You will say to me, "The waves bow under my hand . . .
Where will we live tomorrow . . . what is this land?"

"The night waves are pale," I will say,
"From the island I love we are still far away.

"Close your weary eyes from the voyage and abide
Sleep as in your room closed from noises outside . . .

"Like in an orchard a woman who smiles,
Happiness awaits us on this fragrant isle.

"Cover your pale face with your red hair.
The hour is calm and the peaceful sea is there.

"Don't worry about anything . . . I am aware
Of the risks of the sea and the winds, my fair . . ."

Under the protection of the silver crescent moon,
You will sleep until the approach of the dawn.

The beaches will mark on the horizon gray borders of sand,
. . . Your eyes will open upon the sea's expanse.

You will ask me, not without a little fear,
About the mysterious chants that will reach your ear.

You will say, blushing naively at the noises,
"Nothing is as moving as these unknown voices.

"Their sweet breath cools my weary face like a fan,
But the dawn is still dark and I do not understand.

"Will our black destiny be able to ignore us
At the height of this fearful morning I see before us?"

I will reply, closing your lips with a kiss:
"Happiness is over there . . . But we must take the risk . . .

"Over there, we will hear the supreme music . . .
And, see, we are landing on the island of magic . . ."

COME, GODDESS OF KUPROS . . .

"Come, Goddess of Kupros, and delicately pour
in the gold cups nectar mixed with joy."
–Sappho

My pride has known only reproach and insult,
Inaccessible glory laughs and teases from afar . . .
Since the black laurel will never gird my brow,
Fill the cup and pour me some joy!

I will crown myself with vines, toward dusk.
Thanks to the gracious wine that sings in the marrow,
I will see myself walk toward the blue and be seated
Among the Gods, before a banquet of stars.

Pour the wine of Cyprus and the wine of Lesbos,
Whose hot languor smiles and insinuates itself,
And, the hour being sacred to the red Dionysus,
Take the fragrant lilac and dance, fiery and nude.

I drink of summer, the song of cicadas and fruits,
The flowers and the sun in the hollow of the amphora;
For the festive night is brief among nights
And the divine branch of the vine wilts with the dawn.

MOORISH NIGHT

The night is fashioned with an art so subtle
Similar to a marvelous palace of Boabdil.

The fountain recites its monotonous rhythms
And the silver yew trees stand as white columns.

In the garden, as conquering king, weary and dismal,
The past wraps itself in meditation and keeps vigil.

The sky, where the light shines brilliant ebony,
Is a ceiling of cedar, of pearl, and of ebony.

By this night of love, my desire approaches less
The pure, radiant water stream than it does the cyprus.

None-the-less I love the nightingale's élan,
And, more beautiful than a poem, these fountains.

Come in these walls, to your caprice I surrender,
Zoraida, my lover for all times, and forever.

All along these warm pathways, let us revive,
The languid *ghuzlas* and the women veiled from sight.

And let us dream of an incendiary love,
Trembling with fatal victory, and fever in the blood.

Ma maïtresse! While the moment is yet prolonged,
Let us wander, fingers clasped, in the Alhambra of the song.

WAITING

In this room where memories of confessions disappear,
The jasmine scent of yesterday has strayed . . .
For you alone am I clothed and arrayed
And for you alone have I let down my hair.

I have chosen my jewels . . . have they some hope to please?
In my anxious heart something has been quelled . . .
How do I appear to you and what will you tell,
As you cross my twilight doorway, *mon amie?*

Some violets and sea grasses will be raining through
The violet-colored and soft green stained glass . . .
I savor the ideal anguish of awaiting the gladness
Which comes only when evening draws due.

In silence, I wait for the moment of my desires . . .
The night passes, trailing its cloak, dark and clear . . .
My unlimited soul seems sparse in the air . . .
It is warm tonight: and look–the moon rises.

MEMORIES ARE IN CLUSTERS . . .

This is the amorous hour when the Siren sings . . .
Memories are in clusters that one unstrings.

The silence is like the echo of a rhyme,
And I turn to look at better times,

Toward her who today has my kiss importune,
Her who was my Loreley, my flower of the moon.

During the day I can forget her, but at night,
She rises, so very blond, with her face all light . . .

And I feel myself to be less strong, less serene . . .
This is the amorous hour when the Sirens sing.

Her lovely changing eyes are like water reflected . . .
In dreams, the past always seems more attractive.

When I dream, all the past is changed . . .
I see her letting her hair down in disarray.

When my heart fills with burning at the coming of night,
I forget how much her laugh was in spite.

The crescent moon splits through the clouds' lining . . .
This is the amorous hour when the Sirens sing.

When the looming shadow fills my weary breast,
I feel no happiness is worth the bitter past.

I know how false are the kisses you share,
But I know that tears are also good, O *chère!*

The precious past is a treasure buried deep . . .
Sometimes, I fear nothing save obscurity.

Memories are in clusters that one unstrings.
This is the loving hour when the Sirens sing . . .

YOU FOR WHOM I WROTE

You for whom I wrote, O *belles jeunes femmes!*
You alone whom I loved, will you reread my verse
By future mornings snowing on the universe,
And by future nights of roses and flames?

Will you dream among the charming disarray
Of your disheveled hair, your undone dresses:
"This woman, through joyful times and distresses,
Has carried love through her eyes and lips in this way."

Pale and breathing your flesh scented and lovely,
Will you say, in the magical evocation of night:
"This woman had the fire which eluded me in flight . . .
Why isn't she alive! She could have loved me . . ."

BY FUTURE NIGHTS

No! by future nights of roses and flames,
Mysterious like the Hindu temples,
No one will know my name and none among you
Will retell my verse, O beautiful young women!

None of you will have the charming caprice
Of regretting the love of an unreachable friend,
And of naming, so desirous and pale,
The imperious kiss of my loving lips.

You will search for love, fresh and perfumed,
Turning your irresolute step toward the future,
And none among you will remember me any more
Me, that you would have loved so solemnly . . .

THE PILLORY

For a long time, I was nailed to the pillory,
And some women, seeing me suffering, laughed.

Then, some men took mud in their hands
With which to spatter my temple and cheeks.

The sobs welled up in me, swelling like waves,
But my pride made me choke back the tears.

No one said, "She is perhaps less evil than
We suspect, she is perhaps a poor soul."

The square was public and everyone had come,
And the women laughed in their naive way.

They tossed fruits back and forth to the tune of songs,
And the wind brought to me the sound of their words.

I felt the violent anger steal over me.
Silently, I learned to hate them.

Their insults cut deep, like the thorns of a nettle . . .
When they finally cut me loose, I left.

I went away at the mercy of the wind, and since then
My face is like the face of one dead.

VANQUISHED

The sunset is comparable to the death of a poet . . .
Ah! The weight of years and of lived fantasy!
Here, I taste in peace the hour of defeat,
For the pitiable night is the friend of the vanquished.

My verses have not attained a calm excellence,
I know it now, and no one will read them ever . . .
All I have left are the moon and the close silence,
And the lilies, and above all, the woman I loved . . .

At least, I will have known the splendor without limit
Of color, of line, of flair . . .
I will have lived my life much as one recites
A poem, with art and tenderness and care.

My hands keep the fragrance of beautiful hair.
Let them bury me with my memories, as
One buried with the queens their jeweled finery . . .
I will carry my joy and worry to the other side . . .

Isis, I have prepared the funeral bark
Filled with flowers, spices, and aromatics,
And whose sail unfurls like a shroud . . .
The rowing rituals are ready . . . it is getting late . . .

Under the august protection of your wings,
O Goddess! I will go to meadows without spring . . .
I will leave amid the farewell odes,
On the current wider and blacker than the Nile.

And let my heart be heavy in your just balance,
When I arrive before the fatal throne
Where the black silence is full of vigilance,
And where the Gods with jackal heads serve.

Isis, let me rejoin, in the empty plains,
The obscure poets who know the insults
And who pass, singing their unknown refrains
In the leaden evening that weighs on their brows . . .

THE WORLD IS A GARDEN

The world is a garden of pleasure and death,
Where the shade under the blue leaves seems to wait,
Where the rose is plucked with the noise of ashes,
Where the perfume of lilies is spontaneous and strong.

Amid the new lilies and supreme roses,
We mingle our secrets with the sobs of old . . .
The world is a garden where everything dies,
The poppies, the rosemary, the sage, and even we.

Laughter is hidden everywhere; we feel running
Along the ground, the invisible feet of the breezes,
And we ramble in this garden, infatuated
And fervent, knowing we too must die.

We follow at random our dreams, I lightly
Touch your neck, and your eyes are a sleeping lake.
The sun regards us with the eyes of a friend,
And we do not wonder about the flight of time.

We walk slowly and our shadow follows us . . .
The wind whistles with a long drawn-out shiver . . .
We do not talk of our certain death,
Have we forgotten the approach of night? . . .

INTERIOR

In my soul has flourished the miracle of the rose.
To shelter this, let us keep the doors closed.

I defend my happiness, as one does her treasures,
Against outside noises and the harsh looks of others.

The curtains are drawn on the fragrant silence,
Where the even course of times passes with nonchalance.

Not the slightest breath to make the mimosa tremble
On whose branches a flight of songbirds assembles.

Our room seems to be an immobile garden
Where wandering perfumes come to find asylum.

My existence is like a voyage *accompli*
It is calm, it is refuge, it is obscurity.

To keep this peace fused with glimmers of rose,
O my serenity! Let us keep the doors closed.

The lamp keeps watch over books asleep on bookends,
The fire dances, the furniture surrounds us like friends.

I no longer know the cold outlook of the street
Where each one passes with jaded, rushing feet.

I no longer know if ill is spoken, if we're
The topic still . . . words no longer hurt us here.

Your hair is more beautiful than an autumn forest,
And your careful art weaves braids down your breast.

Yes, the whispers have lost all their malice,
And the hatred of others is no longer a curse.

Your green dress shivers like grasses growing wild,
Love, and your eyes mirror the land and countryside.

Who would come to trouble us, we who are so far
From men? Two children left unnoticed there.

Far from the pavement's turbulence which fades the rose,
Where the raillery chafes–let us stay behind closed doors . . .

HERE IS MY SICKNESS

Among my faded lilies, I muse that it was you
Who gave me my worst broken heart of love, Venice!
You betrayed me like a lover, and conquered me,
Taking my strength, my dreams, and my trust.

I look for nothing more in Venice: the elation
Of noble palaces is no longer in me; the banal song
Of the gondoliers makes me hate the Grand Canal,
And I no longer hope to love the *Dogaresse.*

Here is my sickness: it is negligible and profound.
Rendered indifferent to the beauty that I love,
I wander carrying the eternal mourning of myself,
Because I wear no laurels round my head.

YOU, FATHER ODIN

The winter wind surges out, audacious and strong,
Like the Vikings, in one of their noble rages.
The tempest has blown the secular pines
And the waves have leapt forth . . . Come, my Gods of the North!

Your eyes have the glint of boreal steel,
Chasms are for you easy paths to walk,
And you are big and graceful like the pines,
O masters of cold skies and loyal races!

My Gods of the North, hardy and blond, awake
From your long sleep in the high snows,
And sound your call across the plains
Where the howl of the wolves is prolonged all night.

Come, my Gods of the North, with your warlike faces,
You, our Father Odin and Freya, of the golden hair
Full of fragrances, and you, valorous Thor,
You, Frigga, so willful, and you, my Valkyries!

Listen to me, my Gods, like the clear mornings:
I am a daughter of your venerable poets,
Of those who praise you, standing before the tables
Where the heroes drink the mead of the banquets.

Come, my powerful Gods, because our winter draws near,
We are going to laugh with the joyous storms,
We will fell the oaks spared by the years,
And the mountains will tremble in their very hearts of stone.

We will walk with our triumphant feet on the seas,
We will rejoice in the dance of the waves;
For us, the fog will come alive with vague forms,
And for us the wake of the lightning will shine.

The gulls will shriek at us and at the storm
That we carry in the hollow of our hands . . .
For now one can hear the superhuman combat
And the cries of the fallen on the pale bank.

Now, my Gods, how you laugh as in times of old
And how the eagle turns above its nest.
We have unchained the pack of thunder,
And the cliffs have recognized our voices.

The air will listen to our wild music
And the rebellious skies will bend with our effort . . .
Come to me who awaits you, my Gods of the North!
I am the daughter of the heroic ancient poets . . .

OTHER PUBLICATIONS OF THE NAIAD PRESS

THE LATECOMER by Sarah Aldridge. A Novel. 107 pages.
ISBN 0-930044-00-2 $5.00

TOTTIE by Sarah Aldridge. A Novel. 181 pages.
ISBN 0-930044-01-0 $4.50

CYTHEREA'S BREATH by Sarah Aldridge. A Novel. 240 pages.
ISBN 0-930044- 02-9 $5.00

SPEAK OUT, MY HEART by Robin Jordan. A Novel. 148 pages.
ISBN 0-930044-03-7 $4.00

LESBIANA by Barbara Grier. iv, 309 pages.
ISBN 0-930044-05-3 $5.00

LOVE IMAGE by Valerie Taylor. A Novel. 168 pages.
ISBN 0-930044-08-8 $4.50

THE MUSE OF THE VIOLETS by Renée Vivien. Translated by Margaret Porter and Catharine Kroger. Poetry. xiv, 70 pages.
ISBN 0-930044-07-X $4.00

ALL TRUE LOVERS by Sarah Aldridge. A novel. 292 pages.
ISBN 0-930044-10-X $6.75

BERRIGAN by Gingerlox. A Novel. 172 pages.
ISBN 0-930044-09-6 $5.50

A WOMAN APPEARED TO ME by Renée Vivien. Translated by Jeannette H. Foster. Introduction by Gayle Rubin. xxxi, 65 pages.
ISBN 0-930044-06-1 $5.00

RETREAT: AS IT WAS by Donna J. Young. A Novel. 112 pages.
ISBN 0-930044-12-6 $5.00

THE LESBIAN IN LITERATURE. A Bibliography. Compiled by Gene Damon, Jan Watson and Robin Jordan. 96 pages.
ISBN 0-930044-04-5 $7.00

THE NAIAD PRESS, INC.
7800 WESTSIDE DRIVE
WEATHERBY LAKE, MISSOURI 64152

Mail Orders Welcome
Please Include 15% Postage